TABLE OF C

D0832145

➤-0-◄

CHAPTER   **PAGE #**

Unless otherwise indicated, all Scripture quotations are taken from the King James Version of the Bible.
7 Hidden Keys to Favor, Seeds of Wisdom on Favor, Vol 17 · ISBN 1-56394-113-9/ B-119 · Copyright © 2003 by **MIKE MURDOCK**
All publishing rights belong exclusively to Wisdom International
Publisher/Editor: Deborah Murdock Johnson
Published by The Wisdom Center · 4051 Denton Hwy. · Ft. Worth, Texas 76117
1-817-759-BOOK · 1-817-759-0300
You Will Love Our Website...! www.TheWisdomCenter.tv

Accuracy Department: To our Friends and Partners...We welcome any comments on errors or misprints you find in our book...Email our department: AccuracyDept@thewisdomcenter.tv. Your aid in helping us excel is highly valued.

Uncommon Men
Will Always Celebrate
Uncommon Favor.

-MIKE MURDOCK

1

Any Uncommon Success Will Require Uncommon Favor From Someone

Favor Is The Secret To Uncommon Success.

Favor Is The Difference Between Your Present And Your Future. Favor does not go to those who need it but to those who *value* it.

Favor creates envy. In Joseph's life we see that Favor stirred anger toward him.

Favor will cost you! When you receive Favor you will also experience attack.

Why should you desire Favor? Because you will succeed more quickly with Favor than you will without it.

Every success story contains the Memory of Favor.

Lee Iacocca writes in *Straight Talk* about the Favor that came from his mentor.

Bill Gates, the wealthiest man in America, discusses how he, as a college student, wanted an opportunity to experiment and try something new. He received Favor!

You cannot work hard enough to get everything you deserve. You cannot work long enough to be debt-free. It will require Uncommon Favor to take giant steps into an Uncommon Dream. "The Lord thy God shall bless thee in all thine increase, and in all the works of thine hands," (Deuteronomy 16:15).

Many Do Not Realize That They Are Desperately In Need Of Favor. The people of Nineveh did not realize they needed Favor until Jonah cried out in judgment.

Uncommon Men Are Humble Enough To Pursue Favor. "Then Daniel went in, and desired of the king that he would give him time, and that he would shew the king the interpretation," (Daniel 2:16).

Pursuing Favor With God Qualifies You To Receive Favor. You Have No Right To Anything You Have Not Pursued. "Ye have not because ye ask not," (James 4:2). David sought Favor. "Make Thy face to shine upon Thy servant: save me for Thy mercies' sake," (Psalm 31:16). "The young lions do lack, and suffer hunger: but they that seek the Lord shall not want any good thing," (Psalm 34:10). "He shall pray unto God, and He will be favourable unto him," (Job 33:26). "And Jehoahaz besought the Lord, and the Lord hearkened unto him," (2 Kings 13:4).

Uncommon Favor Should Be Pursued, Requested And Celebrated. When the servant of Abraham knelt and asked God to show him Favor, it was appropriate.

God Is The Source Of Favor. He responds to faith and pursuit. Within hours, Rebekah was en route back to Isaac because of the Favor of God.

Any Uncommon Success Will Require Uncommon Favor From Someone.

2

THE DIVINE PURPOSE OF FAVOR IS TO ENABLE YOU TO ACHIEVE YOUR ASSIGNMENT

Wise Men Study The Law Of Favor.

14 Facts You Should Remember When You Desire Favor

1.   Favor Is A Gift From God. What is Favor? Favor Is Not An Accident, But A Deliberate Design By God To Reward You For Acts Of Obedience Invisible To Others. "If ye be willing and obedient, ye shall eat the good of the land," (Isaiah 1:19).

2.   Favor Is When God Causes Someone To Desire To Become A Problem-Solver In Your Life. It may be a relative, your boss or a stranger. According to the Scripture, God is the Catalyst for linking you to the Golden Connection with someone who blesses you. "And the sons of strangers shall build up thy walls, and their kings shall minister unto thee:...that men may bring unto thee the forces of the Gentiles, and that their kings may be brought," (Isaiah 60:10-11). "...that the mountains might flow down at thy presence," (Isaiah 64:1).

3.   Favor Is An Attitude Of Goodness Toward You, Not An Exchange Or Payment For Something You Have Done. The world uses "favors" as a substitute for Favor. Favors usually are actions designed to manipulate. "My son, if sinners entice thee, consent thou not," (Proverbs 1:10). "For the lips of a strange woman drop as an honeycomb, and her mouth is smoother than oil: But her end is bitter as wormwood, sharp as a twoedged sword. Her feet go down to death; her steps take hold on hell," (Proverbs 5:3-5).

A congressman may say to a lobbyist, "I will push this bill through if you will give me $25,000 for another project." That is an exchange. It is a transaction. You intimidate and obligate others through favors, not Favor. That is the satanic substitution for the Divine Plan of Favor. You will always resent anyone you owe.

Satan has always attempted to imitate God. He envies the success of God, the strength of God and the love that God has generated toward Himself. So, he emulates God.

4.   Favor Is The Divine Way To Success.

5.   Favor Is An Attitude Designed To Reveal The Heart. "O satisfy us early with Thy mercy; that we may rejoice and be glad all our days. Make us glad according to the days wherein Thou hast afflicted us, and the years wherein we have seen evil. Let Thy work appear unto Thy servants, and Thy glory unto their children. And let the beauty of the Lord our God be upon us: and establish Thou the work of our hands upon us; yea, the work of our hands establish Thou it," (Psalm 90:14-17).

6.   Favor Is An Exception To The Rule, Not A Normality. Millions struggle without seeing significant progress. "Except the Lord build the house, they labour in vain that build it," (Psalm 127:1).

7. Favor Is The Willingness, Desire And Participation Of Someone To Help You Advance Or Obtain Something You Want. Noah obtained protection through the Favor of God. Jonathan showed Favor to David and David showed Favor to Mephibosheth, his son.

8. Favor Is A Current, Always Moving Toward You Or Away From You. "And the angel said unto her, Fear not, Mary: for thou hast found favour with God. And Mary said, Behold, the handmaid of the Lord; be it unto me according to thy word. And the angel departed from her," (Luke 1:30,38).

9. Favor Is A Gift From God To Enable You To Achieve Your Assignment. Mordecai knew this and told Esther, "...thou art come to the kingdom for such a time as this?" (Esther 4:14).

10. Favor With Others Is Necessary To Complete Your Assignment From God. Moses realized this to enable him to do what God had told him to do. "...and in the hearts of all that are wise-hearted I have put wisdom, that they may make all that I have commanded thee," (Exodus 31:6).

11. Favor Is Proof Of The Love Of God.

12. Favor Will Increase Dramatically When You Aggressively Cooperate With The Laws Of God. "And Moses said unto the Lord, See, Thou sayest unto me, Bring up this people: and Thou hast not let me know whom Thou wilt send with me. Yet Thou hast said, I know thee by name, and thou hast also found grace in My sight. Now therefore, I pray thee, if I have found grace in Thy sight, shew me now Thy way, that I may know Thee, that I may find grace in Thy sight: and consider that this nation is Thy people.

And He said, My presence shall go with thee, and I will give thee rest," (Exodus 33:12-14).

13. Wise Hearts Search For Opportunities To Sow Favor. "A good man sheweth favour, and lendeth: he will guide his affairs with discretion," (Psalm 112:5). "The just man walketh in his integrity: his children are blessed after him," (Proverbs 20:7).

14. Any Good Seed Guarantees Eventual Favor...Even Years After It Is Planted. The king could not sleep. So, he read. Then he remembered a good deed was unrewarded.

So he had Mordecai rewarded for stopping the assassination attempt. Haman had to celebrate it publicly. "Then took Haman the apparel and the horse, and arrayed Mordecai, and brought him on horseback through the street of the city, and proclaimed before him, Thus shall it be done unto the man whom the king delighteth to honour," (Esther 6:11).

The Divine Purpose Of Favor Is To Enable You To Achieve Your Assignment.

≈ 3 ≈

ATTITUDE AND PROTOCOL DECIDE THE FLOW OF FAVOR INTO YOUR LIFE

Favor Is Not A Mere Miracle But A Reward.

Your life can overflow today with Favor greater than any past experience you can recall. "And Jesus increased in wisdom and stature, and in favour with God and man," (Luke 2:52).

32 Ways To Unleash Uncommon Favor In Your Life

1.   Wisdom Will Increase Favor.   "Now therefore hearken unto Me, O ye children: for blessed are they that keep My ways. Hear instruction, and be wise, and refuse it not. Blessed is the man that heareth Me, watching daily at My gates, waiting at the posts of My doors. For whoso findeth Me findeth life, and shall obtain favour of the Lord," (Proverbs 8:32-35).

2.   Diligence Creates Favor. "The soul of the diligent shall be made fat," (Proverbs 13:4). "He that gathereth by labour shall increase," (Proverbs 13:11).

3.   An Understanding Heart Attracts Favor.   Understanding people and their needs. Understanding a teacher, an instructor or a mentor.

"Good understanding giveth favour," (Proverbs 13:15).

**4.	Appropriate And Right Words Often Generate Favor From Those Around You.** "Death and life are in the power of the tongue," (Proverbs 18:21). "Righteous lips are the delight of kings; and they love him that speaketh right," (Proverbs 16:13).

**5.	Humility Generates Favor.** "The fear of the Lord is the instruction of wisdom; and before honour is humility," (Proverbs 15:33).

**6.	An Uncommon Skill Or Anointing Often Creates Favor.** "The king answered unto Daniel, and said, Of a truth it is, that your God is a God of gods, and a Lord of kings, and a revealer of secrets, seeing thou couldst reveal this secret. Then the king made Daniel a great man, and gave him many great gifts, and made him ruler over the whole province of Babylon, and chief of the governors over all the wise men of Babylon," (Daniel 2:47-48).

**7.	Repentance Brings Favor.** The prodigal son discovered this. "And when he came to himself, he said, How many hired servants of my father's have bread enough and to spare, and I perish with hunger! I will arise and go to my father, and will say unto him, Father, I have sinned against heaven, and before thee, And am no more worthy to be called thy son: make me as one of thy hired servants. And he arose, and came to his father. But when he was yet a great way off, his father saw him, and had compassion, and ran, and fell on his neck, and kissed him," (Luke 15:17-20).

**8.	Favor Increases When You Associate With People Of Integrity.** Boaz had a great reputation for integrity.

Ruth gleaned in his field.

That association brought blessing to all involved.

9. Favor Comes When You Solve A Problem During A Crisis. Daniel interpreted the king's dream before all the wise men were going to be killed. His promotion was inevitable. "For this cause the king was angry and very furious, and commanded to destroy all the wise men of Babylon. And the decree went forth that the wise men should be slain; and they sought Daniel and his fellows to be slain. Then Daniel went in, and desired of the king that he would give him time, and that he would shew the king the interpretation," (Daniel 2:12-13, 16).

10. Favor Can Come When God Reminds Someone Of Something Good You Have Done. The king was reminded that Mordecai had not been rewarded for revealing the plot to assassinate the king. The king scheduled a parade for him! "And the king said, What honour and dignity hath been done to Mordecai for this? Then said the king's servants that ministered unto him, There is nothing done for him," (Esther 6:3).

"And Mordecai went out from the presence of the king in royal apparel of blue and white, and with a great crown of gold, and with a garment of fine linen and purple: and the city of Shushan rejoiced and was glad," (Esther 8:15).

11. Obedience To God Guarantees Favor. "Ye are cursed with a curse: for ye have robbed Me, even this whole nation. Bring ye all the tithes into the storehouse, that there may be meat in Mine house, and prove Me now herewith, saith the Lord of hosts, if I will not open you the windows of heaven, and pour you out a blessing, that there shall not be room enough to receive it. And I will rebuke the devourer for your sakes, and he shall not destroy the fruits of your ground; neither shall your vine cast her fruit before the time in the field, saith the Lord of hosts," (Malachi 3:9-11).

12. Uncommon Achievement Attracts Uncommon Favor. The Queen of Sheba brought gifts to Solomon because of his *achievement.* "And when the Queen of Sheba had seen the wisdom of Solomon, and the house that he had built, And the meat of his table, and the sitting of his servants, and the attendance of his ministers, and their apparel; his cupbearers also, and their apparel; and his ascent by which he went up into the house of the Lord; there was no more spirit in her. And she gave the king an hundred and twenty talents of gold, and of spices great abundance, and precious stones: neither was there any such spice as the Queen of Sheba gave King Solomon," (2 Chronicles 9:3-4, 9).

13. A Good Attitude Often Influences Favor. "...a broken and a contrite heart, O God, Thou wilt not despise," (Psalm 51:17).

Nabal, Abigail's husband, acted foolishly toward David, but because she intervened wisely, David showed Favor and mercy.

Two thieves were crucified with Jesus. One received mercy *because of his attitude* toward Christ. The other was eternally lost. Attitude Affects Favor.

14. Favor Comes When You Solve A Problem More Quickly Than Others Are Willing To Solve It. When Nabal insulted David, Abigail took swift action. "When Abigail saw David, she *hasted...* and fell before David on her face, and bowed herself to the ground," (1 Samuel 25:23). "Whatsoever thy hand findeth to do, do it with thy might," (Ecclesiastes 9:10).

15. Favor Emerges When You Solve A Problem Cheerfully. "For it is God which worketh in you both to will and to do of His good pleasure. Do all things *without murmurings* and disputings," (Philippians 2:13-14). "A *merry* heart doeth good like a medicine: but a broken spirit drieth the bones," (Proverbs 17:22). "Go thy way, eat thy bread with joy, and drink thy wine with a merry heart; for God now accepteth thy works," (Ecclesiastes 9:7).

16. Favor Often Flows The Moment Others Discern The Supernatural Presence Of The Holy Spirit Operating In Your Life. Consider Joseph. "And Pharaoh said unto Joseph, See, I have set thee over all the land of Egypt. And Pharaoh took off his ring from his hand, and put it upon Joseph's hand, and arrayed him in vestures of fine linen, and put a gold chain about his neck; And he made him to ride in the second chariot which he had; and they cried before him, Bow the knee: and he made him ruler over all the land of Egypt. And Pharaoh said unto Joseph, I am Pharaoh, and without thee shall no man lift up his hand or foot in all the land of Egypt," (Genesis 41:41-44).

17. Integrity Guarantees Favor. "Let not mercy and truth forsake thee: bind them about thy neck; write them upon the table of thine heart: So shalt thou find favour and good understanding in the sight of God and man," (Proverbs 3:3-4).

18. Excellence Attracts Favor. Excellence begins with attentiveness to detail. "Finally, brethren, whatsoever things are true, whatsoever things are honest, whatsoever things are just, whatsoever things are pure, whatsoever things are lovely, whatsoever things are of good report; if there be any virtue, and if there be any praise, think on these things. Those things, which ye have both learned, and received, and heard, and seen in me, do: and the God of peace shall be with you," (Philippians 4:8-9).

19. Respecting Authority Unleashes Favor Into Your Life. "Remember them which have the rule over you, who have spoken unto you the word of God: whose faith follow, considering the end of their conversation," (Hebrews 13:7).

"Let every soul be subject unto the higher powers. For there is no power but of God: the powers that be are ordained of God. Whosoever therefore resisteth the power, resisteth the ordinance of God: and they that resist shall receive to themselves damnation. For rulers are not a terror to good works, but to the evil. Wilt thou then not be afraid of the power? do that which is good, and thou shalt have praise of the same," (Romans 13:1-3).

20. Honoring Your Parents Guarantees Lifelong Favor From God. Parents are keys to Uncommon Favor from God. Disobedient children are ignorant of God and the Law of Favor and how it works. "Honour thy father and thy mother, as the Lord thy God hath commanded thee; that thy days may be prolonged, and that it may go well with thee, in the land which the Lord thy God giveth thee," (Deuteronomy 5:16).

21. Increasing Your Knowledge Of God Will Increase Your Favor With God. God responds to pursuit. "Then shall ye call upon Me, and ye shall go and pray unto Me, and I will hearken unto you. And ye shall seek Me, and find Me, when ye shall search for Me with all your heart," (Jeremiah 29:12-13). "...but the people that do know their God shall be strong, and do exploits," (Daniel 11:32).

22. Favor Comes When You Serve Someone Who Is Highly Favored Of God. Ruth received Favor from Boaz because he saw her serve Naomi.

Pharaoh loved Joseph. When Joseph's brothers and families came, they all received gifts of real estate.

23. Favor Will Increase When You Solve A Problem Others Are Unable To Solve. The king was in torment. Nobody could interpret his dream. Daniel did what others could not do. Favor was his reward! "The king answered unto Daniel, and said, Of a truth it is, that your God is a God of gods, and a Lord of kings, and a revealer of secrets, seeing thou couldst reveal this secret. Then the king made Daniel a great man, and gave him many great gifts, and made him ruler over the whole province of Babylon, and chief of the governors over all the wise men of Babylon," (Daniel 2:47-48).

24. Your Favor Will Increase When You Follow An Instruction From A Wise Mentor. Naomi advised Ruth to stay in the fields of Boaz. "And Naomi said unto Ruth her daughter in law, It is good, my daughter, that thou go out with his maidens, that they meet thee not in any other field. So she kept fast by the maidens of Boaz to glean unto the end of barley harvest and of wheat harvest; and dwelt with her mother in law," (Ruth 2:22-23).

Ruth followed Naomi's instruction and ultimately

became the wife of Boaz.

25. Diplomacy And Gracious Responses Birth Favor. "Thou art fairer than the children of men: grace is poured into thy lips: therefore God hath blessed thee for ever," (Psalm 45:2).

26. Wise Use Of Your Gifts And Skills Will Unlock Favor Toward You. Joseph interpreted dreams. "And Pharaoh said unto Joseph, I have dreamed a dream, and there is none that can interpret it: and I have heard say of thee, that thou canst understand a dream to interpret it. And Joseph answered Pharaoh, saying, It is not in me: God shall give Pharaoh an answer of peace," (Genesis 41:15-16).

"And Pharaoh said unto Joseph, Forasmuch as God hath shewed thee all this, there is none so discreet and wise as thou art: Thou shalt be over my house, and according unto thy word shall all my people be ruled: only in the throne will I be greater than thou," (Genesis 41:39-40).

27. Your Appearance Influences Your Favor With Others. When the king *saw* Esther he extended Favor toward her. "Esther put on her royal apparel... And it was so, when the king saw Esther the queen standing in the court, that she obtained favour in his sight: and the king held out to Esther the golden sceptre that was in his hand. So Esther drew near, and touched the top of the sceptre," (Esther 5:1-2).

28. Honoring Your Boss Guarantees Favor From God. "Servants, be obedient to them that are your masters according to the flesh, with fear and trembling, in singleness of your heart, as unto Christ; Knowing that whatsoever good thing any man doeth, the same shall he receive of the Lord, whether he be bond or free," (Ephesians 6:5,8).

"And Joseph found grace in his sight, and he served him: and he made him overseer over his house, and all that he had he put into his hand," (Genesis 39:4).

29. Favor Increases When You Stop A Tragedy Or Solve A Problem For Somebody. Joseph prevented a national crisis through his feed-the-hungry program. Paul on the island brought the miracle of healing to the father of Publius.

30. Gifts That Reveal True Appreciation Are Often Keys To Unlocking Favor With Others. "A man's gift maketh room for him, and bringeth him before great men," (Proverbs 18:16).

31. Favor Often Emerges When Your Intercessors Pray For You. Peter experienced this. He was in prison, but *the church prayed.* God became involved. The doors of the prison opened. Peter was released (see Acts 12:2).

32. Dependability And Loyalty Guarantee Favor With Your Employer. "Most men will proclaim every one his own goodness: but a faithful man who can find?" (Proverbs 20:6, also see Proverbs 28:20).

Attitude And Protocol Decide The Flow Of Favor Into Your Life.

Favor Can Turn
Tragedy Into Triumph
Within Moments.

-MIKE MURDOCK

One Day Of Favor Is Worth A Lifetime Of Labor

Favor Is The Golden Room Of Miracles.

Favor Is The Greatest Harvest You Can Receive From God.

16 Rewards Of Favor

1. Favor Can Instantly Stop A Tragedy In Your Life. It moved Joseph from the prison to Pharaoh's palace in a single day (see Genesis 41:39-40). Esther had Favor with the king and saved an entire nation.

2. Favor Is Often The Only Exit From A Place Of Captivity And Bondage. Joseph knew this. He requested Favor from the butler. Eventually it came.

3. Favor Can Make You Wealthy In A Single Day. Ruth experienced this. "So Boaz took Ruth, and she was his wife," (Ruth 4:13). The wealth of Abraham was transferred to Rebekah through Isaac in a single day.

4. Favor Can Silence A Lifetime Enemy Forever. Haman was hung after the king showed Esther and Mordecai uncommon Favor.

5. Favor Can Make You A Household

Name In 24 Hours. The king chose Esther to be his queen and a nobody became a somebody in a single day (see Esther 2:16).

    6.   **Favor Can Double Your Financial Worth In The Midst Of Your Worst Tragedy.** It happened to Job. "...the Lord gave Job twice as much as he had before. So the Lord blessed the latter end of Job more than his beginning," (Job 42:10, 12).

    7.   **Favor Can Accelerate The Timetable Of Your Assignment And Destiny.** Joseph became Prime Minister within 24 months...even after a false accusation.

    8.   **Favor Can Create Instant Access To Uncommon Leaders Or Mentors.** Daniel knew this. Daniel was able to motivate and get in the good graces of the leader sent by the king to kill the wise men of Babylon. "Therefore Daniel went in unto Arioch, whom the king had ordained to destroy the wise men of Babylon: he went and said thus unto him; Destroy not the wise men of Babylon: bring me in before the king, and I will shew unto the king the interpretation," (Daniel 2:24).

    Daniel received *instant access* to the king. "Then Arioch brought in Daniel before the king in haste, and said thus unto him, I have found a man of the captives of Judah, that will make known unto the king the interpretation," (Daniel 2:25).

    9.   **Favor From God Often Increases Favor With Enemies.** "When a man's ways please the Lord, He maketh even his enemies to be at peace with him," (Proverbs 16:7).

    10. **Favor Causes A Flow Of Wealth And Influence.** "Therefore thy gates shall be open

continually; they shall not be shut day nor night; that men may bring unto thee the forces [wealth] of the Gentiles, and that their kings may be brought," (Isaiah 60:11).

11. Favor Can Cause Instant Restoration Of Everything Satan Has Ever Stolen From You. Job received twice what he had before. David was restored to kingship. Abraham moved in Favor with the king and Abimelech gave him many gifts. "And Abimelech took sheep, and oxen, and menservants, and womenservants and gave them unto Abraham, and restored him Sarah his wife. And Abimelech said, Behold, my land is before thee: dwell where it pleaseth thee," (Genesis 20:14-15).

12. Favor Can Cause A Barren Woman To Give Birth To A Child. "And God said unto Abraham, As for Sarai thy wife, thou shalt not call her name Sarai, but Sarah shall her name be. And I will bless her, and give thee a son also of her: yea, I will bless her, and she shall be a mother of nations; kings of people shall be of her," (Genesis 17:15-16).

"And God remembered Rachel, and God hearkened to her, and opened her womb. And she conceived, and bare a son; and said, God hath taken away my reproach," (Genesis 30:22-23).

13. Favor Is Instant Credibility Without The Cost Of Years And Money.

14. Favor Grants Protection During Storms Of Criticism.

15. Favor Positions You For Every Harvest And Gift.

16. Favor Will Produce More Than A Lifetime Of Labor. Ruth was a peasant woman.

She worked hard for her living. She toiled, she sweated and remained poor. But in a single day, Boaz accepted her as his wife.

Favor moved Joseph from the prison to the palace of Pharaoh in one day. Nothing is more glorious or more miraculous. Nothing else can create ecstasy like a single experience of Favor.

Favor is the secret, hidden and unspoken dream of every human living today. We strive for it, pray for it and even beg for it.

Favor can turn tragedy into triumph within moments.

One Day Of Favor Is Worth A Lifetime Of Labor.

True Gratitude For Favor Received Will Guarantee Your Success

Even Fools Receive A Measure Of Favor.

You have already received the Gift of Favor many times whether you realize it or not. "But let all those that put their trust in Thee rejoice: let them ever shout for joy, because Thou defendest them: let them also that love Thy name be joyful in Thee. For Thou, Lord, wilt bless the righteous; with favor wilt Thou compass him as with a shield," (Psalm 5:11-12).

"Blessed is the people that know the joyful sound: they shall walk, O Lord, in the light of Thy countenance. In Thy name shall they rejoice all the day: and in Thy righteousness shall they be exalted. For Thou art the glory of their strength: and in Thy favour our horn shall be exalted. For the Lord is our defence; and the Holy One of Israel is our king," (Psalm 89:15-18).

Stop for a moment. Identify the Dominant Source of Favor in your life. Have you written a note of *appreciation*? Have you sown Favor into your own family?

▶ *What You Fail To Recognize, You Stop Celebrating.*

▶ *What You Stop Celebrating, You Stop Rewarding.*

▶ *Anything Unrewarded Will Exit Your Life.*

Favor Celebrated Becomes Favor Perpetuated And Repeated. Examine the life of Abigail. "So David received of her hand that which she had brought him, and said unto her, Go up in peace to thine house; see, I have hearkened to thy voice, and have accepted thy person. And when the servants of David were come to Abigail to Carmel, they spake unto her, saying, David sent us unto thee, to take thee to him to wife," (1 Samuel 25:35, 40).

Note the secret of Ruth. "Then she fell on her face, and bowed herself to the ground, and said unto him, Why have I found grace in thine eyes, that thou shouldest take knowledge of me, seeing I am a stranger? Then she said, Let me find favour in thy sight, my lord; for that thou hast comforted me, and for that thou hast spoken friendly unto thine handmaid, though I be not like unto one of thine handmaidens," (Ruth 2:10, 13).

Ask yourself these questions:

1. Who are the top 10 who have made the greatest deposits in your life?

2. How have you honored those who have shown you Favor?

True Gratitude For Favor Received Will Guarantee Your Success.

≈ 6 ≈

Favor Can Stop As Quickly As It Began

Never Trivialize Favor.

It is *not* guaranteed. It is *not* eternal. It is a *gift*.

The Israelites expressed this. There rose up one who "knew not Joseph." "And the children of Israel were fruitful, and increased abundantly, and multiplied, and waxed exceeding mighty; and the land was filled with them. Now there arose up a new king over Egypt, which knew not Joseph. And he said unto his people, Behold, the people of the children of Israel are more and mightier than we: Therefore they did set over them taskmasters to afflict them with their burdens," (Exodus 1:7-9, 11).

Favor Is Often Ignored Or Taken For Granted.

How many times has someone paid for a meal and no one really took the time to say, "Thank you"? Untrained children gladly eat a meal and then get upset when their mother asks them to "do the dishes".

11 Things That Can Stop The Flow Of Favor Into Your Life

1. Favor Stops When You Trivialize Your Access To Wise Counsel. "My people are destroyed for lack of knowledge: because thou hast rejected knowledge, I will also reject thee, that thou shalt be no priest to Me: seeing thou hast forgotten the law of thy God, I will also forget thy children," (Hosea 4:6).

"A wise man will hear, and will increase learning; and a man of understanding shall attain unto wise counsels," (Proverbs 1:5).

2.   The River Of Favor Will Dry Up When God Observes Greed. "Will a man rob God? Yet ye have robbed Me. But ye say, Wherein have we robbed Thee? In tithes and offerings. Ye are cursed with a curse: for ye have robbed Me, even this whole nation," (Malachi 3:8-9). It is a tragedy, an absurdity and futility to try to breathe Favor into a family or an individual whom God has chosen to curse because of their greed.

3.   Favor Stops When Gratitude Stops. "Because that, when they knew God, they glorified Him not as God, neither were thankful," (Romans 1:21).

4.   Favor Will Stop When You Deliberately Ignore An Instruction From God. Saul ignored the instructions of Samuel to destroy King Agag and all the Amalekites. Favor stopped. Saul was removed from the throne and David became the king (read 1 Samuel 15:9-11, 26).

5.   The Flow Of Favor Stops Because Of An Attitude Of Arrogance And Self-Sufficiency. When Nebuchadnezzar sneered at the authority of God because of his uncommon success, God permitted him to live like a beast in the field until his humility returned (see Daniel 5:20-21).

6.   Any Broken Or Ignored Law Of God Stops Favor Toward You From God. "They are not humbled even unto this day, neither have they feared, nor walked in My law, nor in My statutes, that I have set before you and before your fathers. Therefore thus saith the Lord of hosts, the God of Israel; Behold, I will set My face against you for evil, and to cut off all Judah," (Jeremiah 44:10-11).

7. Any Ignored Opportunity To Solve A Problem Stops Favor. You will lose Favor the moment you ignore a problem you are capable and called to solve for someone. "But whoso hath this world's good, and seeth his brother have need, and shutteth up his bowels of compassion from him, how dwelleth the love of God in him?" (1 John 3:17).

8. Favor Stops When You Follow Wrong Counsel. Rehoboam followed wrong counsel. "And the king answered the people roughly, and forsook the old men's counsel that they gave him; And spake to them after the counsel of the young men," (1 Kings 12:13-14). Tragedy was inevitable.

9. Favor Stops When You Associate With Wrong People. The children of Korah were destroyed like he was. "And the earth opened her mouth, and swallowed them up, and their houses, and all the men that appertained unto Korah, and all their goods. They, and all that appertained to them, went down alive into the pit, and the earth closed upon them: and they perished from among the congregation," (Numbers 16:32-33).

10. Favor Stops When You Dishonor Your Parents. "A foolish son is a grief to his father, and bitterness to her that bare him," (Proverbs 17:25). "A wise servant shall have rule over a son that causeth shame, and shall have part of the inheritance among the brethren," (Proverbs 17:2).

11. Favor Stops When You Ignore Wise Counsel. "They would none of My counsel: they despised all My reproof," (Proverbs 1:30).

Favor Can Stop As Quickly As It Began.

Your Willingness
    To Sow Favor Determines
Your Worthiness
    To Receive Favor.

-MIKE MURDOCK

7

Every Seed Of Favor You Sow Schedules A Wave Of Favor In Your Own Future

Every Day Is An Opportunity To Sow Favor.

Favor Is A Seed That Anyone Can Sow Into The Life Of Another.

It does not require money, nor genius nor uncommon skill. It requires love, attentiveness and time. "Knowing that whatsoever good thing any man doeth, the same shall he receive of the Lord, whether he be bond or free," (Ephesians 6:8).

"And the Lord turned the captivity of Job, when he prayed for his friends: also the Lord gave Job twice as much as he had before," (Job 42:10).

"For by grace are ye saved through faith; and that not of yourselves: it is the gift of God: Not of works, lest any man should boast. For we are His workmanship, created in Christ Jesus unto good works, which God hath before ordained that we should walk in them," (Ephesians 2:8-10).

When You Sow The Seeds Of Favor Consistently, You Will Consistently Reap The Harvest Of Favor. Erratic Seeds produce erratic Harvests. Seeds of Love, Patience and Forgiveness will begin to grow in your own life.

The Harvest Of Favor Is Reaped Over A Period Of Time. Mordecai was celebrated years after he aborted the assassination attempt of the king. Jesus "grew in favor with God and man," (Luke 2:52).

Your Willingness To Sow Favor Is A Photograph Of Your Thankful Heart. Thankful people celebrate Favor. "And they, continuing daily with one accord in the temple, and breaking bread from house to house, did eat their meat with gladness and singleness of heart, Praising God, and having favour with all the people," (Acts 2:46-47).

The Thankful Know That Favor Is A Gift To Be Given, Not Demanded. Esther is an example. "And said, If it please the king, and if I have found favour in his sight, and the thing seem right before the king, and I be pleasing in his eyes, let it be written to reverse the letters devised by Haman the son of Hammedatha the Agagite, which he wrote to destroy the Jews which are in all the king's provinces," (Esther 8:5).

Uncommon Men Always Sow Uncommon Favor Toward Others. "A good man sheweth favour, and lendeth: he will guide his affairs with discretion," (Psalm 112:5).

David sowed into Absalom.

Abraham sowed into Lot.

Joseph sowed into Potiphar.

Uncommon Men Always Sow Uncommon Favor Into Uncommon Women. Boaz sowed into Ruth's life (see Ruth 2:13-14).

Jesus Sowed Forgiveness Into The Life Of An Adulteress. "When Jesus had lifted up Himself, and saw none but the woman, He said unto her, Woman, where are those thine accusers? hath no man condemned thee?" (John 8:10).

Every Seed Of Favor You Sow Schedules A Wave Of Favor In Your Own Future.

DECISION

Will You Accept Jesus As Your Personal Savior Today?

The Bible says, "That if thou shalt confess with thy mouth the Lord Jesus, and shalt believe in thine heart that God hath raised Him from the dead, thou shalt be saved," (Romans 10:9).

Pray this prayer from your heart today!

"Dear Jesus, I believe that You died for me and rose again on the third day. I confess I am a sinner...I need Your love and forgiveness...Come into my heart. Forgive my sins. I receive Your eternal life. Confirm Your love by giving me peace, joy and supernatural love for others. Amen."

Clip and Mail

DR. MIKE MURDOCK

is in tremendous demand as one of the most dynamic speakers in America today.

More than 16,000 audiences in 39 countries have attended his Schools of Wisdom and conferences. Hundreds of invitations come to him from churches, colleges and business corporations. He is a noted author of over 200 books, including the best sellers, *The Leadership Secrets of Jesus* and *Secrets of the Richest Man Who Ever Lived*. Thousands view his weekly television program, *Wisdom Keys with Mike Murdock*. Many have attended his Schools of Wisdom that he hosts in major cities of America.

❏ Yes, Mike! I made a decision to accept Christ as my personal Savior today. Please send me my free gift of your book, *31 Keys to a New Beginning* to help me with my new life in Christ.

NAME _____ BIRTHDATE _____

ADDRESS _____

CITY _____ STATE _____ ZIP _____

PHONE _____ E-MAIL _____

Mail form to:
The Wisdom Center · 4051 Denton Hwy. · Ft. Worth, TX 76117
1-817-759-BOOK · 1-817-759-0300
You Will Love Our Website...! www.TheWisdomCenter.tv

DR. MIKE MURDOCK

1 Has embraced his Assignment to Pursue...Proclaim...and Publish the Wisdom of God to help people achieve their dreams and goals.

2 Began full-time evangelism at the age of 19, which has continued since 1966.

3 Has traveled and spoken to more than 16,000 audiences in 39 countries, including East and West Africa, the Orient and Europe.

4 Noted author of over 200 books, including best sellers, *Wisdom For Winning, Dream Seeds* and *The Double Diamond Principle.*

5 Created the popular *Topical Bible* series for Businessmen, Mothers, Fathers, Teenagers; *The One-Minute Pocket Bible* series, and *The Uncommon Life* series.

6 The Creator of the Master 7 Mentorship System.

7 Has composed more than 5,700 songs such as "I Am Blessed," "You Can Make It," "God Rides On Wings Of Love" and "Jesus, Just The Mention Of Your Name," recorded by many gospel artists.

8 Is the Founder of The Wisdom Center, in Fort Worth, Texas.

9 Has a weekly television program called *Wisdom Keys With Mike Murdock.*

10 Has appeared often on TBN, CBN, BET and other television network programs.

11 Has had more than 3,000 accept the call into full-time ministry under his ministry.

THE MINISTRY

1 **Wisdom Books & Literature** - Over 200 best-selling Wisdom Books and 70 Teaching Tape Series.

2 **Church Crusades** - Multitudes are ministered to in crusades and seminars throughout America in "The Uncommon Wisdom Conferences." Known as a man who loves pastors he has focused on church crusades for 40 years.

3 **Music Ministry** - Millions have been blessed by the anointed songwriting and singing of Mike Murdock, who has made over 15 music albums and CDs available.

4 **Television** - *Wisdom Keys With Mike Murdock,* a nationally-syndicated weekly television program.

5 **The Wisdom Center** - The Church and Ministry Offices where Dr. Murdock speaks weekly on Wisdom for The Uncommon Life.

6 **Schools of The Holy Spirit** - Mike Murdock hosts Schools of The Holy Spirit in many churches to mentor believers on the Person and Companionship of The Holy Spirit.

7 **Schools of Wisdom** - In many major cities Mike Murdock hosts Schools of Wisdom for those who want personalized and advanced training for achieving "The Uncommon Life."

8 **Missions Outreach** - Dr. Mike Murdock's overseas outreaches to 39 countries have included crusades in East and West Africa, South America, the Orient and Europe.

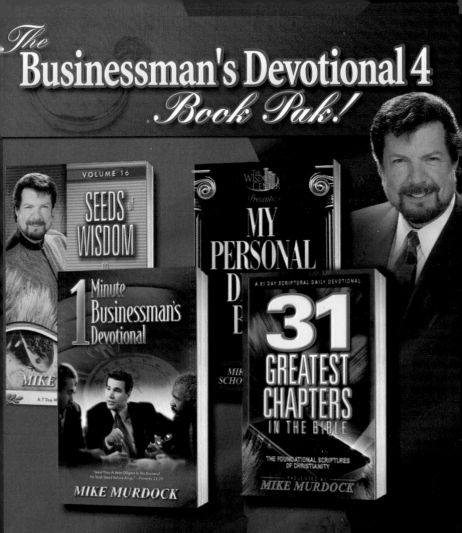

The Businessman's Devotional 4 *Book Pak!*

VOLUME 16
SEEDS of WISDOM

THE WISDOM CENTER presents:
MY PERSONAL D... B...

1 Minute Businessman's Devotional
"Seest Thou A Man Diligent In His Business? He Shall Stand Before Kings" - Proverbs 22:29
MIKE MURDOCK

A 31 DAY SCRIPTURAL DAILY DEVOTIONAL
31 GREATEST CHAPTERS IN THE BIBLE
THE FOUNDATIONAL SCRIPTURES OF CHRISTIANITY
PRESENTED BY **MIKE MURDOCK**

1 Seeds of Wisdom on Problem-Solving/<u>Book</u> (32pg/B-118/$5)

2 My Personal Dream Book/<u>Book</u> (32pg/B-143/$5)

3 1 Minute Businessman's Devotional
/<u>Book</u> (224pg/B-42/$12)

4 31 Greatest Chapters In The Bible
/<u>Book</u> (138pg/B-54/$10)

The Wisdom Center
The Businessman's Devotional 4 Book Pak!
Only **$20** $32 Value
PAK-22
Wisdom Is The Principal Thing

*Each Wisdom Book may be purchased separately if so desired.

Add 10% For S/H

THE WISDOM CENTER 4051 Denton Highway • Fort Worth, TX 76117
1-817-759-BOOK
1-817-759-0300

You Will Love Our Website...!
TheWisdomCenter.tv A

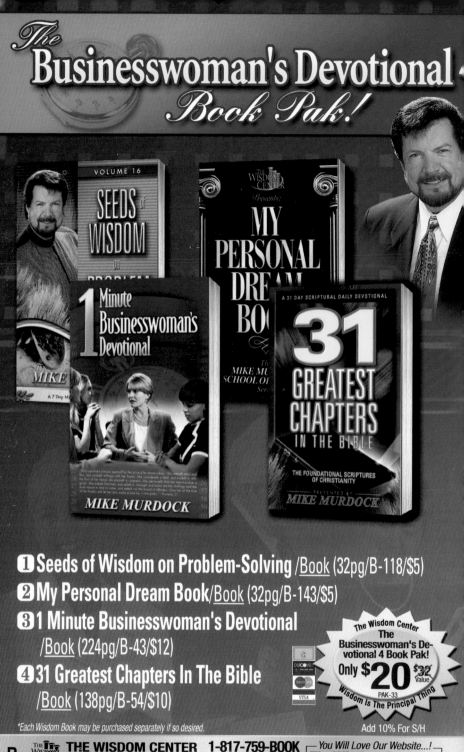

The Businesswoman's Devotional Book Pak!

❶ Seeds of Wisdom on Problem-Solving /Book (32pg/B-118/$5)

❷ My Personal Dream Book/Book (32pg/B-143/$5)

❸ 1 Minute Businesswoman's Devotional
/Book (224pg/B-43/$12)

❹ 31 Greatest Chapters In The Bible
/Book (138pg/B-54/$10)

The Wisdom Center
The Businesswoman's Devotional 4 Book Pak!
Only **$20** $32 Value
PAK-33
Wisdom Is The Principal Thing

Each Wisdom Book may be purchased separately if so desired.

Add 10% For S/H

Crisis 7
BOOK PAK!

DR. MIKE MURDOCK

❶ The Survival Bible/<u>Book</u> (248pg/B-29/$10)

❷ Wisdom For Crisis Times/<u>Book</u> (112pg/B-40/$9)

❸ Seeds of Wisdom on Motivating Yourself/<u>Book</u> (32pg/B-171/$5)

❹ Seeds of Wisdom on Overcoming/<u>Book</u> (32pg/B-17/$3)

❺ Seeds of Wisdom on Warfare/<u>Book</u> (32pg/B-19/$3)

❻ Battle Techniques For War-Weary Saints/<u>Book</u> (32pg/B-07/$5)

❼ Seeds of Wisdom on Adversity/<u>Book</u> (32pg/B-21/$3)

The Wisdom Center
Crisis 7 Book Pak!
Only $30 $38 Value
WBL-25
Wisdom Is The Principal Thing

Add 10% For S/H

Quantity Prices Available Upon Request

*Each Wisdom Book may be purchased separately if so desired.

 THE WISDOM CENTER 4051 Denton Highway • Fort Worth, TX 76117
1-817-759-BOOK
1-817-759-0300

You Will Love Our Website...!
TheWisdomCenter.tv

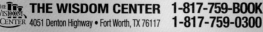

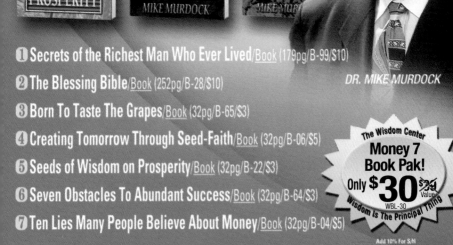
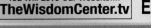

Spirit Music.

The Mike Murdock Music Library

LOVE SONGS TO THE HOLY SPIRIT

Written In The Secret Place

TS-59

THE HOLY SPIRIT HANDBOOK

What You Need To Know About Your Daily Companion, The Holy Spirit

Songs...

1. A Holy Place
2. Anything You Want
3. Everything Comes From You
4. Fill This Place With Your Presence
5. First Thing Every Morning
6. Holy Spirit, I Want To Hear You
7. Holy Spirit, Move Again
8. Holy Spirit, You Are Enough
9. I Don't Know What I Would Do Without You
10. I Let Go (Of Anything That Stops Me)
11. I'll Just Fall On You
12. I Love You, Holy Spirit
13. I'm Building My Life Around You
14. I'm Giving Myself To You
15. I'm In Love! I'm In Love!
16. I Need Water (Holy Spirit, You're My Well)
17. In The Secret Place

18. In Your Presence, I'm Always Changed
19. In Your Presence (Miracles Are Born)
20. I've Got To Live In Your Presence
21. I Want To Hear Your Voice
22. I Will Do Things Your Way
23. Just One Day At A Time
24. Meet Me In The Secret Place
25. More Than Ever Before
26. Nobody Else Does What You Do
27. No Walls!
28. Nothing Else Matters Anymore (Since I've Been In The Presence Of You Lord)
29. Nowhere Else
30. Once Again You've Answered
31. Only A Fool Would Try (To Live Without You)
32. Take Me Now
33. Teach Me How To Please You

34. There's No Place I'd Rather Be
35. Thy Word Is All That Matters
36. When I Get In Your Presence
37. You're The Best Thing (That's Ever Happened To Me)
38. You Are Wonderful
39. You've Done It Once
40. You Keep Changing Me
41. You Satisfy

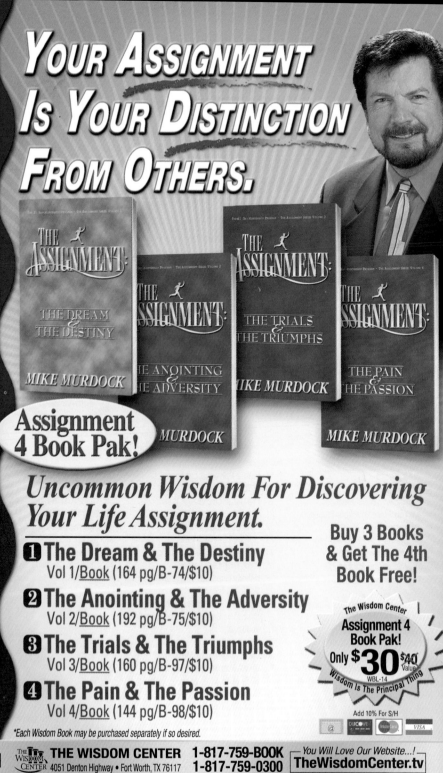

101 Wisdom Keys That Have Most Changed My Life.

THE LAWS OF LIFE SERIES

The **SCHOOL** *of* **WISDOM**

SERIES 2

101 WISDOM KEYS THAT HAVE MOST CHANGED MY LIFE

MIKE MURDOCK

The **Law of Recognition**

Discovering the Gifts, Opportunities, & Relationships That God Has Already Placed In Your Life

999.9 FINE

MIKE MURDOCK

TS-42

101 WISDOM KEYS THAT HAVE MOST CHANGED MY LIFE

DR. MIKE MURDOCK

School of Wisdom #2 Pak!

▶ What Attracts Others Toward You
▶ The Secret Of Multiplying Your Financial Blessings
▶ What Stops The Flow Of Your Faith
▶ Why Some Fail And Others Succeed
▶ How To Discern Your Life Assignment
▶ How To Create Currents Of Favor With Others
▶ How To Defeat Loneliness
▶ 47 Keys In Recognizing The Mate God Has Approved For You
▶ 14 Facts You Should Know About Your Gifts And Talents
▶ 17 Important Facts You Should Remember About Your Weakness
▶ And Much, Much More...

The Wisdom Center
School of Wisdom #2 Pak!
Only **$30** $40 Value
PAK002
Wisdom Is The Principal Thing

Add 10% For S/H

DISCOVER   MasterCard   VISA

THE WISDOM CENTER
4051 Denton Highway • Fort Worth, TX 76117
1-817-759-BOOK
1-817-759-0300
You Will Love Our Website...!
TheWisdomCenter.tv

Financial $ecrets.

THE 31 DAY MENTORSHIP PROGRAM
31 REASON$
PEOPLE DO NOT RECEIVE THEIR
FINANCIAL HARVE$T
MIKE MURDOCK

The Wisdom Center
Buy One... Receive The Second One FREE!
Wisdom Is The Principal Thing

VIDEO
7 KEYS
to
1000
TIMES MORE
The Lord God Of Your Fathers Make You A Thousand Times So Many More As You Are, And Bless You, As He Hath Promised You!
Deuteronomy 1:11
MIKE MURDOCK

VI-17

VI-16

Your Financial World Will Change Forever.

Video 2-Pak!

▸ 8 Scriptural Reasons You Should Pursue Financial Prosperity

▸ The Secret Prayer Key You Need When Making A Financial Request To God

▸ The Weapon Of Expectation And The 5 Miracles It Unlocks

▸ How To Discern Those Who Qualify To Receive Your Financial Assistance

▸ How To Predict The Miracle Moment God Will Schedule Your Financial Breakthrough

▸ Habits Of Uncommon Achievers

▸ The Greatest Success Law I Ever Discovered

▸ How To Discern Your Place Of Assignment, The Only Place Financial Provision Is Guaranteed

▸ 3 Secret Keys In Solving Problems For Others

The Wisdom Center
Video 2-Pak!
Only $**30** $60 Value
VIPAK-01
Wisdom Is The Principal Thing

Add 10% For S/H

J **THE WISDOM CENTER** 4051 Denton Highway • Fort Worth, TX 76117 **1-817-759-BOOK** **1-817-759-0300** *You Will Love Our Website...!* **TheWisdomCenter.tv**

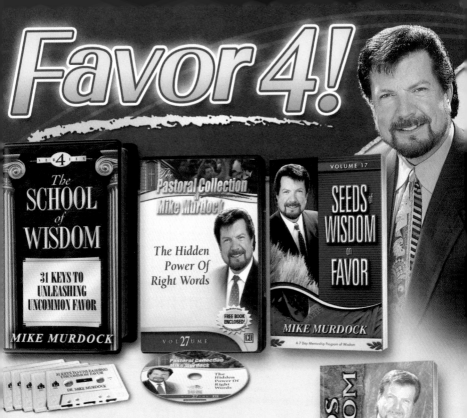

Favor 4!

This Collection Of Wisdom Will Change The Seasons Of Your Life Forever!

1 The School of Wisdom #4 / 31 Keys To Unleashing Uncommon Favor...Tape Series/6 Cassettes (TS-44/$30)

2 The Hidden Power Of Right Words... The Wisdom Center Pastoral Library/CD (WCPL-27/$10)

3 Seeds of Wisdom on Favor/Book (32pg/B-119/$5)

4 Seeds of Wisdom on Obedience/Book (32pg/B-20/$3)

*Each Wisdom Product may be purchased separately if so desired.

The Wisdom Center
Favor 4 Collection!
Only $**35** Value
PAK-12
Wisdom Is The Principal Thing

Add 10% For S/H

The CRISIS COLLECTION

Wisdom For Crisis Times — Master Keys For Success In Times Of Change — MIKE MURDOCK

SEEDS of WISDOM on MOTIVATING YOURSELF — MIKE MURDOCK

Wisdom For Crisis Times — Master Keys For Success In Times Of Change — MIKE MURDOCK

You Get All 6 For One Great Price!

❶ 7 Keys For Surviving A Crisis/<u>DVD</u> (MMPL-04D/$10)
❷ You Can Make It!/<u>Music CD</u> (MMML-05/$10)
❸ Wisdom For Crisis Times/<u>6 Cassettes</u> (TS-40/$30)
❹ Seeds of Wisdom on Overcoming/<u>Book</u> (32pg/B-17/$3)
❺ Seeds of Wisdom on Motivating Yourself/<u>Book</u> (32pg/B-171/$5)
❻ Wisdom For Crisis Times/<u>Book</u> (112pg/B-40/$9)

Also Included... Two Free Bonus Books!

*Each Wisdom Product may be purchased separately if so desired.

The Wisdom Center
The Crisis Collection
Only $**40** $67 Value

Wisdom Is The Principal Thing

Add 10% For S/H

L — THE WISDOM CENTER — 4051 Denton Highway • Fort Worth, TX 76117

1-817-759-BOOK
1-817-759-0300

You Will Love Our Website...!
TheWisdomCenter.tv

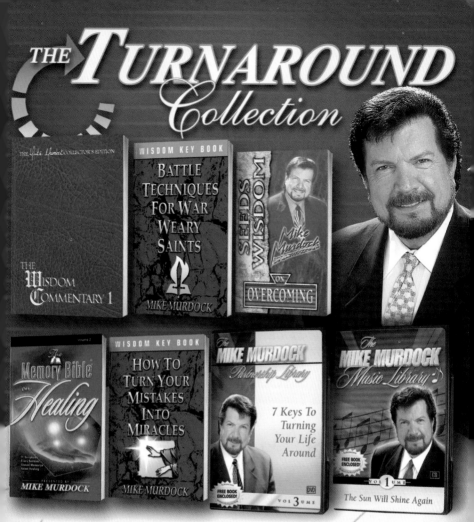

THE TURNAROUND Collection

1. **The Wisdom Commentary Vol. 1**/Book (256pg/52 Topics/B-136/$20)
2. **Battle Techniques For War-Weary Saints**/Book (32pg/B-07/$5)
3. **Seeds of Wisdom on Overcoming**/Book (32pg/B-17/$3)
4. **The Memory Bible on Healing**/Book (32pg/B-196/$3)
5. **How To Turn Your Mistakes Into Miracles**/Book (32pg/B-56/$5)
6. **7 Keys To Turning Your Life Around**/DVD (MMPL-03D/$10)
7. **The Sun Will Shine Again**/Music CD (MMML-01/$10)

Each Wisdom Product may be purchased separately if so desired.

The Wisdom Center
The Turnaround Collection
Only $40 $56 Value
PAK-15
Wisdom Is The Principal Thing

Add 10% For S/H

THE WISDOM BIBLE

Partnership Edition

Over 120 Wisdom Study Guides Included Such As:

- ▶ *10 Qualities Of Uncommon Achievers*
- ▶ *18 Facts You Should Know About The Anointing*
- ▶ *21 Facts To Help You Identify Those Assigned To You*
- ▶ *31 Facts You Should Know About Your Assignment*
- ▶ *8 Keys That Unlock Victory In Every Attack*
- ▶ *22 Defense Techniques To Remember During Seasons Of Personal Attack*
- ▶ *20 Wisdom Keys And Techniques To Remember During An Uncommon Battle*
- ▶ *11 Benefits You Can Expect From God*
- ▶ *31 Facts You Should Know About Favor*
- ▶ *The Covenant Of 58 Blessings*
- ▶ *7 Keys To Receiving Your Miracle*
- ▶ *16 Facts You Should Remember About Contentious People*
- ▶ *5 Facts Solomon Taught About Contracts*
- ▶ *7 Facts You Should Know About Conflict*
- ▶ *6 Steps That Can Unlock Your Self-Confidence*
- ▶ *And Much More!*

Your Partnership makes such a difference in The Wisdom Center Outreach Ministries. I wanted to place a Gift in your hand that could last a lifetime for you and your family...**The Wisdom Study Bible.**

40 Years of Personal Notes...this Partnership Edition Bible contains 160 pages of my Personal Study Notes...that could forever change your Bible Study of The Word of God. This **Partnership Edition...**is my personal **Gift of Appreciation** when you sow your Sponsorship Seed of $1,000 to help us complete The Prayer Center and TV Studio Complex. An Uncommon Seed Always Creates An Uncommon Harvest!

Mike

Thank you from my heart for your Seed of Obedience (Luke 6:38).